Apocalyptic Visions

(Revised Edition)

By Phil Gibson

Copyright © Phil Gibson 2011
Illustrations copyright © Caroline Quin 2011

ISBN 978-1-4478-0570-0

This book is sold subject to the condition that it shall not, by way of trade or otherwise, be lent, resold, hired out, or otherwise circulated without the publisher's prior consent in any form of binding or cover other than that in which it is published and without similar condition, including this condition, being imposed on the subsequent purchaser.

Table of Contents

Forward   4

A Painful truth   6
A Revelation   8
Apocalyptic Vision   9
Billboard Prophet   14
Childish Tears   15
Curtain Call   16
Genesis   17
God Save the Children   18
Hell on Earth   19
Hopeless Glory   20
Letter to Santa   22
Letter to the P.M   24
Listen, Do You Hear Them?   26
Lost   27
Mice or Men?   29
Morbid, Who Me?   31
Morbidity   34
New Life, Old Death   36
One Question, Lord   37
Parasite   41
Peace in Our Time(1992)   44
Poppy Petals   45
Prophet's Lament   46
Savage in a Suit   47
Shell-shocked   50
Terminal Case   52
The Candle   53
The Price of Prosperity   54
Tomorrow's Legacy   56
Two Eyes   58

Also by Phil Gibson   60
Connect online   63

Forward

Some people may think it is a little early to be releasing a Revised Edition of my first collection of poetry and normally I would agree. When I started this project I never intended it as a full revision, just a quick spring clean to tidy up the formatting and iron out a few wrinkles in the punctuation. Then I moved house...

While sorting through boxes unopened since the last move I turned up some old notebooks dating back 20 years containing original draft notes for the title poem, Apocalyptic Vision. These notes yielded 2 complete stanzas not previously published in the 1st Edition, allowing me to present this poem in its original form for the first time in years.

Apocalyptic Vision, the poem, has special significance for me as it was the first. It was written during the winter of 1990-91 as the world held its breath awaiting the inevitability of the 1st Gulf War. At the time I was living in the attic of an isolated tumble-down bungalow on the Lizard Peninsula in Cornwall, struggling to survive on little money and less hope for the future as I mourned a love lost. By night I drank and wandered the rugged Lizard Downs, often finding myself at the cliff top above The Point, by day I slept off the night before. I felt my life could get no lower. Then everything changed...

On a crisp winter's day I aimlessly wandered the streets of Helston during a rare daytime visit to civilization, noticing the shoppers going about their day little more than they noticed me. I was pulled up suddenly by a strange noise that was not so much heard over the bustle that surrounded me as felt under it; a kind of throbbing vibration in my breast and temple that droned on and on, louder and louder. I looked about in confusion to find the source and saw that no-one else was reacting, the crowd simply parted about me with a mutter and a scowl at my obstruction of their vital journey. Slowly my gaze was drawn upwards as I realised the noise came from above, beyond the low hanging blanket of cloud, as comprehension washed over me like cold rain. I was hearing aero-engines, big ones. Some-where high above this small town English street large aircraft droned across the sky, bringing to mind US B-52 heavy bombers en-route to the Persian Gulf. The throbbing reverberation rumbled on, increasing to a dull roar that surely even the most ardent bargain hunter could not ignore, and yet they did, paying more attention to the obvious lunatic staring dumbly at the sky and blocking their path to the sale signs.

At that precise moment I had an epiphany. I immediately purchased a pen and note-book and boarded the first bus home, sketching out the bare bones of the first couple stanzas of my Apocalyptic Vision by the time I reached the bungalow. I retreated to the attic, my garret, and continued to write...

Everything in this collection is a direct expression of that moment...

A Painful Truth

A figure of death
Looms over the land
A nuclear scythe
Is borne in his hand
Wearing a mantle
Of consuming fire
He lights for our world
A funeral pyre

I flee in terror
But find no escape
For all of this land
Shows signs of his rape
Where-ever I go
He is always there
Stripping the land
And leaving it bare

I hear his cruel laughter
A malicious sound
While his victims' corpses
Are thick on the ground
He's dealing out death
And pain on a whim
There can be no way
Of hiding from him

But now I am running
So desperate to hide
For I've glimpsed a truth
I cannot abide
The horror flows through me
For now I can see
There is no escape
This figure is me!

A Revelation

I dreamt I saw the sea on fire
But as the flames began to fade
I saw the self-proclaimed Messiah
He rode a jackass motorcade
Wearing his crown of razor wire
Through green stained blood I saw him wade

A silhouette in the setting sun
Twelve star disciples in his hand
He said His great work had begun
His golden creed spread through the land
The time had come, His will be done
I'd either die or understand

To my mind came a revelation
The present's future past to come
All people of the world, one nation
A view of paradise to some
United in annihilation
All creeds together, every one

Apocalyptic Vision

Our world was dying, slow but sure
Whole species gone forever more
The rivers ran with filth and slime
The heavens stained with soot and grime
The poisoned sea, the barren land
And all this caused by human hand
In man's remorseless quest for power
He pillaged nature's sacred bower
Without a thought where it may lead
His one desire to sate his greed

But still mankind was not content
On self-destruction he seemed bent
As noxious vapours heat the sky
The crops all fail, the cattle die
The deserts grow, the graves do fill
The famines spread and yet man still
Let populations grow unchecked
While bones of folly vultures pecked
As man careered madly on
Not happy 'til his world was gone

Then trouble in the east began
All started by one Arab man
Who saw his neighbours land and wealth
And planned to take them for himself
He sent his troops in without warning
Resistance crushed in just one morning
The nations of the world enraged
In futile talks of peace engaged
To find solutions just and fair
While armies of the world prepare

And so the mighty warlords met
They talked of peace, they smiled and yet
They left that room with war in mind
A reason for it yet to find
Until a fireball in the east
Provoked the slumbering Hebrew beast
Long suffering they could take no more
They gave that Arab his holy war
Star of David burning bright
Set the Arab world alight

The time had come, the war begun
The battle that could not be won
The bells of doom began to toll
As war machines began to roll
And devils laughed and danced with mirth
Hell's fury loosed upon the Earth
As mighty metal beasts that crawl
And spit out fire and death for all
Began their slow futile advance
Began the Reaper's favourite dance

The fires of Hell were put to shame
As the world we knew was set aflame
And as the flames grew ever higher
For the human race, a funeral pyre
Black smoke obscured the noon daylight
The world engulfed in eternal night
By the war foretold by ancient seers
Ignored by man for a thousand years
Too late man sees the truth at last
The Apocalypse has come to pass

Poison and plague rain from the sky
A million men painfully die
Diseases spread throughout the land
Purposely placed by terror's hand
And in response, red buttons pressed
While keys are turned, excuses stressed
Resulting in man's greatest hour
Supreme expression of his power
To end his world by his own hand
In brief memorial mushrooms stand

The fighting stopped, a silence fell
Black rain quenched the fires of hell
The few survivors looked around
And saw the burned and blackened ground
The land was just a wasteland bare
No man or beast was moving there
But peace had come, the war was done
Though neither side had really won
In fact the human race had lost
And few were left to count the cost

But peoples of the world be calm
Your leaders they are safe from harm
Beneath the ground they lie in wait
Like beasts of prey, consumed with hate
And when the land again is green
They will emerge, a sight obscene
To start the human race anew
To take control, the chosen few
They'll lead us as they did before
Along the beaten path to War

Billboard Prophet

The billboard prophet prowls the city streets
He's preaching doom and gloom to all he meets
"Repent you sinners for the end is nigh!"
They hear the prophet`s well known battle cry

He says The Judgement Day is drawing near
But no-one on the street has time to hear
To them their time is measured by its gain
And anyway, this old man is insane

But why does every-body hurry by?
Uneasy glances as they hear his cry
Maybe they don`t think he is such a fool
Could he know something they should all know too?

But he is just an old and lonely man
He has no secret knowledge of life`s plan
He is just a man with opened eyes
Who sees the truth as our world slowly dies

Childish Tears

I can see a child crying
As he hugs his injured knee
And a feeling of such sorrow
Is awakened there in me

I can see the child`s tears
Falling softly to the ground
I can hear his tearful sobbing
And I`m haunted by the sound

For I know a time is coming
When the children all will cry
As they wonder why their parents
Let the world around them die

Curtain Call

The show is coming to an end now
It's time to turn down all the lights
There will be no more sunny days now
There will only be dark endless nights

The curtains will be coming down now
To the silent sound of tears
The orchestra has long been dead now
The audience died through the years

There will be no more cries for encore
And no bouquets thrown on the stage
Because the cast is not there anymore
To see the dawning Golden Age

Despite the Author's best intentions
And of the Director, His Son
The leading man made new inventions
For gain he slaughtered everyone

So all the lights are going dim now
All fading quickly one by one
The Author starts to write again now
Another story has begun

Genesis

There was a time when we weren't here
But then God had a good idea
He took a shapeless lump of clay
And formed this earth in just one day
And when He said, "Let there be light!"
Up popped the sun, all clear and bright
And cast its gold illumination
On God's sparkling new creation

Then He made the waters flow
And caused the trees and grass to grow
He brought forth fish to swim the seas
And fowl to nest within the trees
And called forth beasts to roam the land
All formed from clay by His own hand

But on the sixth and final day
One creative thought did go astray
And where it fell upon the ground
Man sprang up and looked around
He saw this land straight from God's heart
And began to take it all apart

God Save the Children

God save the children
From the troubles of this life
Shield them and protect them
From the heartache and the strife

God save the children
Dry their tears when they cry
When the world mistreats them
Do not turn a blinded eye

God save the children
Cold and lonely in life's rain
Shelter them and feed them
They just don't deserve the pain

God save the children
Do not listen to the lie
Of those who'd exploit them
Do not let the children die

God save the children
All our hopes they will fulfill
Some-one has to save them
As no-body down here will!

Hell on Earth

If there is a Prince of Darkness
And He is alive and well
I'm sure He would be more at home
On earth than down in Hell

Just take a look around you
And I'm sure you will agree
When you open up your eyes
To all the pain and misery

So when the churches try to scare you
With damnation, do not fear
I'm sure Hell must be empty
As the devils are all here

Hopeless Glory

The flag is raised, the cry goes out
"IT'S WAR!" the tabloid headlines shout
The country rallies to the cause
Aggression rips the peaceful gauze

We fight for peace and human rights
We're off to set the world to rights
A chance to revel in the glory
A sequel to the same old story

We see the boys off with loud cheers
Their loved ones shed a few proud tears
But it's a time to celebrate
They're off to crush the ones we hate

But as the troops sail from our shore
We somehow lose touch with the war
Our gallant boys, of course we care
But all the fighting's over there

The gung-ho spirit stays alive
Until the body bags arrive
And when the casualty lists grow
Most people just don't want to know

The wounded, blinded, scarred and maimed
Burnt by our fervour's fire inflamed
The shell-shocked, weary and insane
And countless free from further pain

They've paid the price for you and me
To keep our country's liberty
But now they've no more part to play
Ungratefully we walk away

Letter to Santa

Dear Father Christmas
I do not want lots of gifts
I am not writing to you
With my usual Christmas list

This year it is different
There's just one thing I would like
And it's not a new computer
Or the latest mountain bike

Please Santa can you help me
For I do not want a toy
Could you turn me into some-thing
Other than a little boy

Because every little boy
Grows up and then becomes a man
And it's men who cause the problems
That are ruining God's plan

It's men who kill the animals
And fight in all the wars
In all the bad news I have seen
It's men who are the cause

I haven't got a mummy
And I haven't got a dad
No-one here will miss me
So no-one will be sad

So Santa can you help me
Can you make my wish come true?
Could you turn me into an elf
Then take me home with you?

Letter to the P.M.

Dear mister prime minister
I am not very old
But I'm writing you this letter
Cos it's time that you were told

My daddy doesn't like you
And mummy doesn't too
Cos daddy lost his job last month
And he says it's cos of you

Now mummy's got to find a job
So she can buy us shoes
And daddy now plays cards all night
But all he does is lose

My mummy isn't happy
Cos my daddy couldn't stay
He borrowed some-one's money
And the police took him away

And now we haven't got a house
Cos the bank man took the key
So now we all live in one room
In a smelly B&B

Now I know why daddy hates you
And I hate you just the same
You didn't do your job right
That's why you're the one I blame

Listen, Do You Hear Them?

Listen, do you hear them?
In the quiet of the night
A million souls are crying
As they mourn the fading light
The darkness overwhelms them
As they huddle round the fire
Though they know the Sun is dying
They refuse to light the pyre

Dogmatic arches tumble round them
As they cling to every stone
Though the Advocate is lying
They still hear his words alone
But the shadows whisper to them
From dark reaches of the mind
And the Prophets sadly sighing
To the end he is resigned

Listen, do you hear them?
From dark caverns 'neath the ground
While above the corpses lying
There's no-one to hear the sound
No, there's no-body to hear them
All their pleas fall on dead ears
But they have to keep on trying
Through the swiftly darkening years

Lost

I'm wandering lost
In an alien land
Cast out in a world
I don't understand
Wistfully gazing
Through mist laden eyes
At vitiriol clouds
In thermal glass skies

Pestilent deserts
Stretch mile upon mile
Pockmarked by copses
Of skeletons vile
Blackened and twisted
Limbs reach for the sky
A miasmal breeze
Passes through with a sigh

My eyes start to fill
As onward I roam
Past festering rivers
That bubble and foam
Foul gurgling cocktails
With flotsam of death
Like open-cast sewers
With venomous breath

To the horizon
My stinging eyes gaze
Vast tombstones are rising
Through death dealing haze
Cancerous tumours
Malignant they stand
Belching forth black fumes
To poison the land

I stumble half blind
Now sobbing with grief
My mind in a whirl
Of cruel disbelief
This vision of Hell
Seen blurred by my tears
Will be my own world
Or has been for years

Mice or Men?

You may call this life a rat race
But to me the only rats
Are the ones in spangled uniforms
Or suits and bowler hats

The rest of us are only mice
All chained to life's tread-mill
While the rats ride on the gravy train
And eat and drink their fill

They are living in the manner
They have grown accustomed to
While the masses pay in blood and sweat
For the lifestyle of the few

They enjoy all of life's comforts
Never wanting for their needs
While the masses live in penury
Victims of their leader's greed

To them our fate is just a game
As they play dice with our souls
The masses are expendable
To their power crazy goals

And when the final war arrives
They will be the first to hide
In concrete bunkers down below
While the masses burn outside

Don't you think it's time to show them
Whether we are mice or men?
We should put the rats back in their cage
And then try to start again

Morbid, Who Me?

There is a question
I have been asked
now so many times;
I'm always asked
why do I have to
write depressing rhymes?

These people say
that I should write
of pleasant happy things,
Describing pretty
flowers and
the way the songbird sings.

They ask me why
I cannot write
of love and peace and joy,
Portraying laughing
children playing
with a favourite toy.

They say that I
should tell of all
the beauty of this land,
I try to give
my answer but
they do not understand.

The reason is
so clear to me,
why can't they realise?
I cannot write
these things for then
I would be telling lies.

The sad fact is
this world is full
of hatred, war and pain,
A world in which
the children are
locked up and go insane.

They dug up all
the flowers, shot
the birds out of the sky,
I cannot write
of beauty as
I watch that beauty die.

Morbidity

I have a dream, a fantasy
Where all men live in harmony
An end to pain and enmity
A new birth for humanity

Each day I wake reluctantly
And come back to reality
I look around in misery
And see the true insanity

A world ruled by brutality
Supported by complacency
We're in the grip of tyranny
Choked by our own misanthropy

The masses in obscurity
Condemned to live in poverty
A life of harsh severity
The cruellest immorality

Each day a new atrocity
Will reach new depths of cruelty
We're sinking into savagery
A slow death for humanity

New Life, Old Death

As each new day breaks round the world
A precious plaintive cry is heard
A new life drawing its first breath
Beginning on the road to death

This miracle of life's new birth
Another victim for this earth
And man's depravity run wild
What kind of life for this new child?

For each child born another dies
Murdered by this world of lies
And no-one sees the mother's tears
Or understands her pain of years

So many wasted innocents
Consumed by man's malevolence
But do not fill your heart with scorn
Rejoice; another child is born!

One Question, Lord

Lord, I know I've never prayed
And I really don't know how
But I feel there is a question
That I have to ask you now

The bible says you made this earth
From the void in just six days
Then displayed your love of beauty
In a myriad different ways

You started off creating time
By dividing day from night
And set the eternal cycles
With the darkness and the light

On the next day of creation
Your great wisdom you did show
Dividing vapours up above
From the waters down below

On the third day you continued
Separating land and sea
And set the plants to grow there-in
In a vast abundancy

On the fourth day you decided
On a focus for the light
You made the sun to watch the day
And the moon to rule the night

On the fifth day you created
Fish to swim the lakes and seas
And birds to fly upon the wind
And nest within the trees

On the last day you excelled yourself
Making beasts to roam the land
Be they crawling on their bellies
Or upon their legs to stand

Now, I know you will not like this
But there's something I must say
I think you made a big mistake
On that sixth and final day

It's a shame you were not happy
With the beauty of this land
For you blew it all completely
When you formed from clay a man

On that day you made a monster
Filled with anger, greed and hate
And he set about destroying
All the work you'd done to date

He is killing off your creatures
At a truly frightening speed
And the only reason for it
Is his never ending greed

He pollutes your seas and rivers
And he doesn't seem to care
That the life-style he is living
Is now poisoning the air

In his task he is relentless
Destroying all things in his way
He can now reverse your process
Of creation in a day

If things carry on much longer
It won't matter anymore
That the world is slowly dying
He'll destroy it in a war

So Lord, I now beseech you
Will you listen to my cry?
I only have one question
And that question Lord is Why?

Parasite

Imagine, if you will, our world
As some great beast, in sleep it's curled
It's blood, the rivers deep and long
Its bones, the mountains, proud and strong
Its organs, oceans and the seas
Its lungs, the forests, life they breathe

But as the beast in sleep does lie
It knows not it is doomed to die
For as it slumbers through the years
A tiny parasite appears
It quickly spreads across the beast
And on its life begins to feast

This infestation without sense
Unchecked it grows in virulence
And as the beast sleeps all the while
Pollutes its blood with poisons vile
That flow through hardened arteries
Into the organs of the seas

And still this pestilence was rife
It cut into the lungs of life
But as it ate into the bones
Leeching the minerals from the stones
The beast began to feel the pain
Too late it tried to stir again

With horror then the beast saw all
The carnage caused by pests so small
Like insects on its back they crawled
Like mighty nests their cities sprawled
Like worms they burrowed in its skin
It knew not where it could begin

Within the beast an anger burned
As fiery emotions churned
Erupting as a searing flood
That shook its bones and boiled its blood
The cities burned, the mountains fell
The beast unleashed the gates of hell

But when the smoke of fires cleared
The parasites again appeared
From holes where they had gone to hide
Their heads kept down, the storm to ride
And when the beast did see them there
Its anger died, it knew despair

And so the beast was filled with woe
It mourned itself, its tears did flow
And as it wept the waters rose
Inexorably drowning those
Who'd come to cause it so much pain
Now soon it would be cleansed again

The beast it saw and ceased to weep
Then settled right back down to sleep
Content the parasite was gone
It failed to notice there upon
A mountain stood a group of men
Who planned to start it all again

Peace In Our Time (1992)

To see peace in a modern sense
Just look to Lebanon
In Beirut's battered city streets
The fighting still goes on

In what was Yugoslavia
They're fighting once again
The U.N. called a cease-fire
But their efforts are in vain

And close to home in Belfast
Where the Troubles still go on
Where soldiers armed with empty guns
Face the bullet and the bomb

Religion fights religion
And the Arab fights the Jew
And dogs of war fight every-one
If they are paid their due

And no-one seems contented
Unless settling a score
There's only one more thing to say
Thank god there is no war!

Poppy Petals

Lonely dripping scarlet tears
Spread their stain across the years
Silent rivulets of blood
Go unnoticed in the mud

Blood stained crosses stand in rows
As the single bugle blows
Poppy petals in the breeze
Hide the unseen agonies

By the rusty barbed wire fence
Water fills the empty trench
Where so much young blood was spilt
And yet the guilty feel no guilt

Prophet's Lament

In this world of power gone mad
Alone I sit, forlorn and sad
I see the way that things will go
But wonder if to let man know
The time left to us is so brief
This so called gift brings so much grief

Future events before me lie
I see them all but wonder why
This weighty task was laid on me
Oh how I wish I could be free

Inside I know what I should do
But don't know if I'll bother to
Does mankind deserve to be saved
After the way that he's behaved?
This earth so pure when man first breathed
But now about it death is wreathed

I know that I should make a stand
That I should try to save this land
But will the people heed my cry
Or ridicule me as they die?

Savage in a Suit

You think you are so civilised
But it is time you realised
How easily cracks can appear
In your so finely groomed veneer

We're just a couple of meals away
From anarchy, so experts say
I'm sure you doubt this can be true
So I'll try to enlighten you

The basic instinct in us all
Before which all the others fall
Is that to keep yourself alive
At all costs you have to survive

Imagine now some future date
When all the world's long pent-up hate
Erupts into the final war
The Establishment exists no more

The things you take for granted now
They are no longer there somehow
No petrol for your fancy car
Well, am I getting through so far?

No food will reach your local store
Your power and water flow no more
Gangs and looters roam the night
Now there is no electric light

But things will go from bad to worse
With worthless money in your purse
No matter, there's no food to buy
And anyway, the end is nigh

Soon shortages will start to bite
Out on the streets the people fight
For any food that does arrive
Remember, they have to survive

At first the law enforcers try
But soon they start to wonder why
They bother with a fruitless quest
They're in the same boat as the rest

And that is when the end will start
When our society falls apart
No-one to keep the mob in check
The rats have left the sinking wreck

They talk of concrete jungles now
But they just don't compare somehow
To millions of our charming race
Competing in a real rat race

Countless starving millions dying
On the streets the corpses lying
And those unlucky ones alive
With only one thought, to survive

Could you survive this brave new world
When anarchies flag is unfurled?
Or would you just curl up and die
Cowering as your children cry?

Shell-shocked

My head is throbbing dully
As I slowly come around
And at first I can't remember
Why I'm lying on the ground

But then it all comes back to me
As my mind is clear at last
A deafening explosion
As the ground shook with the blast

I try to look around me
As I peer through the haze
But have to shield my blistered face
A vehicle's ablaze

A twisted hunk of metal
By a hole there in the ground
Then the ringing in my ears stops
And I hear the dreadful sounds

A low and mournful moaning
Punctuated now by screams
The voice of utter terror
Never heard in my worst dreams

I look around in disbelief
At a vision straight from hell
All about me twisted bodies
Lying broken where they fell

The twitching human debris
Writhing, moaning with the pain
As the shocked and stunned survivors
Pick their way through the remains

But there is not one uniform
On the murdered and the slain
Not one of them were paid
To throw their lives away in vain

For this was once a crowded street
Where no-one knew or cared
'Til they became the victims
In a war no-one declared

Terminal Case

Now this really is a most interesting case
But I'm sorry to say we're losing the race
To halt the infection, it's spreading too fast
The way things are going the subject won't last

We're dealing here with a most virulent strain
As you see the life signs are all on the wane
This must be the worst case that we've ever seen
That's why we are keeping it in quarantine

The parasite is quite a devious one
By disguising itself as a symbion
It managed to spread undetected with ease
It just wasn't recognised as a disease

But when it was ready it raised its vile head
From then on the subject was as good as dead
The parasite then launched a ruthless assault
On all natural functions almost without fault

But it multiplies with such alarming speed
Devouring its host with insatiable greed
I'm sorry to say there's no cure we can find
This world has a terminal case of mankind

The Candle

The candle flame is burning bright
A humble source of simple light
And yet this candle wakes in me
A view of our mortality

As I watch the candle burn away
Just as our world burns day by day
Its soot and smoke pollute the air
No-one around me seems to care

Dark shadows dance upon the wall
Like devils come to watch our fall
They gather round the dying flame
And laugh as we apportion blame

And as I watch the flame burn low
With horrid certainty I know
Just like the candle fading fast
Our species reign on earth won't last

The Price of Prosperity

The charges are set
We're ready to blast
There's no need to worry
The mountain will last
This rubble is needed
For factory walls
We've no time to rest
Prosperity calls

Stoke up the furnace
Don't let the fire die
Keep the coal coming
An endless supply
We must keep producing
There's more fuel to burn
The darkness at noon
Is not our concern

There's no time to rest
There're more trees to fell
The more we cut down
The more we can sell
It's all they are good for
They're dead anyway
Soaked in pollution
To wither away

Send out the trawlers
With wall of death nets
There must be an hour
Before the sun sets
We have to work harder
The only solution
There's less fish to catch
That's man's contribution

The pressure is mounting
Our profits are down
There's no time for sleeping
Get up off the ground
There's so little time left
We have to get on
Why is it so dark?
Where has our world gone?

Tomorrow's Legacy

How will you explain to grandchildren to come
Why they cannot go out and play in the sun
Without some kind of ultra-violet screen
How will you explain the plain truth so obscene?

How will you explain why they can't go outside
Without an air filter behind which to hide?
Or maybe it won't be so hard to because
They'll never have known what fresh air really was

How will you explain that it's your legacy
That stops them from taking a dip in the sea?
And will you explain that there once was a time
When all the world's oceans were not lifeless slime?

How will you explain the lost beauty of trees?
How will you describe rustling leaves in the breeze?
When you tell them about living carpets of green
Will they comprehend something they've never seen?

How will you explain to a future grandchild
That animals used to run free in the wild
When he's only seen a selection so few
Who live wretched lives locked away in the zoo?

How will you explain how the world used to be
Before it succumbed to man's insanity?
How will you explain why you stood idly by
And let your grandchildren's inheritance die?

Two Eyes

Two eyes are still closed tightly
To the beauty of this earth
A face still glistens brightly
From the miracle of birth

Two eyes, a flickered movement
As a new life is unfurled
But the wonder of this moment
Is just wasted on this world

Two eyes begin to open
And in wonder gaze around
Youth's bud begins to ripen
As those eyes grow big and round

Two eyes born out of innocence
See the world with rosey hue
Still blind to all the violence
And the evil that men do

Two eyes are filled with anger
As they open to the truth
The mirror holds a stranger
Something missing from their youth

Two eyes now disillusioned
And ashamed of their own kind
In a torment of confusion
Now they wish they were still blind

Two eyes have now grown cynical
Against this world of pain
They've reached and passed life's pinnacle
And soon will close again

Two eyes are quickly dimming
And their light is fading fast
The world about is swimming
As they look into the past

Two eyes now close forever
At their owner's final breath
In that face like wrinkled leather
Lying peacefully in death

Also by Phil Gibson

Beyond the Mask

This collection offers a peek beyond the mask of the author. The glimpse is brief and partial; sometimes sad, sometimes funny, sometimes serious, sometimes whimsical but always candid. Look into my eye, it's time to see what hides down that rabbit hole...

Reviews

A few reviews from Fanstory.com, a review website where writers gather to critique each other's work (listed by fanstory.com username):

Cjvaugn – 5 stars

You caught me from the first line to the last. Compelling and riveting emotion, I liked how you draw us in and take us on the experience...

Take care, CJ

mamonia – 5 stars

Wow! This is some kind of powerful. You really got a rise out of me with the description and imagery of words. Fantastic poetry showing the depth of your feelings and creating a major impact on the reader.

Great

Snowbound – 5 stars

WOW

Dark, demented, delicious. I love the imagery. You take us right into the straight jacket...

SnowBound

The Jumper

I have out-lived my usefulness
Rejected to my loneliness
Discarded here upon the shelf
My only company, myself

It is a dreadful truth to see
To know that no-body wants me
Of this sad fact there is no doubt
Who'd want me now, I'm too worn out

Before me now my life is played
As I sit here with edges frayed
Each fibre of my being stretched
My misery in creases etched

Unravelling, I wonder why
It came to this, I start to cry
I long for peace in endless sleep
With eyes closed, off the cliff I leap

Available from Lulu.com:
http://www.lulu.com/product/paperback/beyond-the-mask/16427554

Connect online

Twitter:
http://twitter.com/#!/PhilG_Poetry

Facebook author page:
http://www.facebook.com/pages/Phil-Gibson-Poetry

Facebook book pages:
Apocalyptic Visions - http://www.facebook.com/ApocalypticVisions
Beyond the Mask - http://www.facebook.com/Beyond.the.Mask

Smashwords:
https://www.smashwords.com/profile/view/philgibson

Phil Gibson Poetry:
http://philgibsonpoetry.co.uk/

Phil's blog:
http://philgibsonpoetrythegarret.blogspot.com/

www.ingramcontent.com/pod-product-compliance
Lightning Source LLC
Chambersburg PA
CBHW061248040426
42444CB00010B/2300